<u>THE NEW FASCISM</u>

1. State and Medicine: where does one end and the other begin?

2. Dark Triad: Manichean, Zoroaster and Star Wars

STATE AND MEDICINE: where does one end and the other begin?

While the concepts of wellness and the present development of medicine into all areas of life is in many ways a welcome development on the other hand it invades individual autonomy. On the basis of professional, a state in fact fairly new to modern societies, perception in the west people can involve themselves in your life. Professional interference modes are due to social change such as the shrinking of families and family life, with outside distractions eminent, as well as family breakdowns.[1] Although the family is still seen as the traditional, emotional and relationship core of society, the state has made continuous inroads.

At some point in life, mainly as a consequence of the breakup of family life and a consequent lack of interest in each other, everyone below a certain income becomes the responsibility of the state. This means care, possible hospitalisation, and submission to medical drugs. Quality of life is unlikely to be sustained and individuals become objects of obedience, their existences subject to record, the

---

[1] Ferguson, D M, et al. A Proportional Hazards Model of Family Breakdown. *Journal of Marriage and Family* Vol. 46, No. 3 (Aug., 1984), pp. 539-549

processing of data, diagnosis and inspection. Data stored on all of us becomes fixed and immutable. Bodies and minds become one; objects of inspection. For many this unremitting reductionism is acceptable as thinking, choice and intentionality become unnecessary.

To what degree are the claims of modern medicine true or are we subject to the effects of propaganda? In *Medicine's Symbolic Reality On a central problem in the philosophy of medicine* Arthur M Kleinman writes of modern medicine as a cultural system in which symbolic meaning plays a part in disease formation, the classification of and cognitive management of disease and treatment. For an example, medicine is often filled with martial or management statements of control. Often the words and phrases employed reflect the hierarchical, political systems in play within medicine itself. *Science*, as an engaged word, is a symbolic indicator of efficacy, which involves the symbolic rejection or putting off of death and in psychiatry represents stasis, exorcism and a thankful return to middleclass norms. A narrative of mind and body is formed that demonstrates the location and power of physical decay through the clinician's forestalling of the inevitable: not quality of life but simply life.

While Michel Foucault[2] held that the clinic is the rationale of medical empiricism (a newly translated Madness and Civilisation covers much more ground than the original 1961 translation), throughout the twentieth century this became as much the General Practioner's surgery situated at the core of the community but representative of an elite group. The doctors, members of an elite, lived and functioned elsewhere and had and have little to do with the community. The surgery was and is the place where treatment and drugs are dispensed, although now it inhabits a business model where treatment becomes a form of economic activity. Treatments that have become increasingly utilitarian fixed to a profit margin; treatments which the community itself does not qualify as effective or ineffective but only the medical profession; patients are objects that receive treatments, failing to engage or be engaged.

---

[2] Foucault, Michel. On Madness and Civilisation:A history of insanity in an age of reason. Psychology Press 2001.

Doctors remain the central actors in medical institutions of all varieties, and are held as largely responsible still for its development even though now they are merely by and large agents for medical bodies and drug companies. Much power is invested in doctors and they remain a cornerstone of government.[3] Like solicitors and barristers, doctors symbolise the nature of professionalism based upon a knowledge base, not skills, and are considered the guardians with autonomous control of the knowledge base. Although instructed as to what is and is not effective treatments they remain a barrier to others acquisition of this knowledge. Doctor's immense control of both medicine and patients is generally ascribed to the growth of capitalism (Weber, neo-Marxism) exemplified by their huge salaries. Doctors are certainly models for middle class lifestyles, status and elite power. They have formed an unchallenged patriarchy or matriarchy.

State within a state

---

[3] Medical Dominance in Britain: Image and Historical Reality. *The Milbank Quarterly*

Vol. 66, Supplement 2: The Changing Character of the Medical Profession (1988), pp. 117-132 (16 pages)

G.V. Larkin writes in *Medical Dominance in Britain: Image and Historical Reality* that the medical profession forms a state within a state with (118) *'either acquired or invested sovereignty.'* He remarks that economics has made headway into their sovereignty but not to any great extent. Psychiatry indeed has retained and spread its dominance over the discourse of human potentiality and patients' lives. As will be seen, psychiatry is effectively as close to being an autonomous state within a state that is possible to be, enjoying not only its own rules but also perceptions. Nevertheless, Larkin specifies that although medical dominance may not have expanded in the United States (sic) it seems to have in the United Kingdom.

Psychiatry anyway remains a special case and should be analysed differently. Freidson specifies that medical dominance is retained through doctors changing the nature of medicine and their part in it. Where psychiatry is concerned, the specialisation changes through its choice of treatments and by altering treatments (from the 1930s shock treatment followed by lobotomy and then drugs) has allowed them to expand their power base as well as remove public and government gaze from the failures of previous treatments. At present, the specialisation is developing the idea of bacteria as the aetiology of mental illness in order to cover up the failure and long term damage to patients of drug treatments. In that way it retains its power even if it does not necessarily expand it.

Eliot Freidson[4] notes the powerful connection of medical authorities to government policies. The closing down of asylums several decades ago provided an opportunity for psychiatry to move into the community out of hospitals and propagate more effectively its ideas and extend even further its treatment tally. The visibility of mental health tropes may be an extension of this. Eliot Freidson[5] qualifies *profession*, especially the medical profession, as within the desire for freedom to act outside of the oversight of laypeople, a position radically emphasised and achieved by psychiatry that insists that no layperson can understand its processes (sic), and within division of labour. Patient problems are re/structured and managed, and a new social reality established. In psychiatry, a patient goes from one reality of family, work, domesticity and responsibility into another

---

[4] *Profession of Medicine*. Harper and Row. 1970, *Professional Dominance,* New York, Dodd: Mead. 1970.
[5] *Profession of medicine: A Study of the Sociology of Applied Knowledge* University of Chicago Press. 1988.

of complete subservience and often complete control by others: of indeed autonomy of some degree to non-existence.

One salient point is that in the United Kingdom the medical profession expanded through the consent of ruling elites who in the past and now were often related to one another. The national state anyway seems to have been sympathetic to enhanced medical authority. In the United Kingdom, medical doctors remain representative of the middle class, with, in the National Health Service their cliental belonging to the lower classes-those with often limited education and a subservient attitude towards doctors.

The National Health Service was probably the first and greatest aid to medical expansion, providing large salaries for doctors as well as enhancing their status. Deeply connected to governments, medical groups blossomed and deepened their power, which prior to the NHS had been less directional and more fragmented.

<u>History</u>

The nature of present medicine, its narrow focus, is a consequence of state involvement with medicine and medical authorities' contradictory desire to limit medicine's range. In the early part of the 20th century, herbalists and osteopaths were denied state registration which meant that neither could apply for state employment. Although both occupations are now not considered genuine medicine by the general public this is mainly due to the activity of medical authorities and the class structure they inhabit. Medically trained members of the Ministry of Health made sure that certain medical treatments were excluded from the public arena but left to the private arena only. Psychotherapy came under the same restrictions, but as much through its own organisational desire not to become another arm of the state,[6] adding to its demotion today in favour of the state financed biological interpretation of mental illness and the use of drugs. Psychotherapists have resisted the data led, quota based, economic mindset of modern medicine, especially psychiatry, for the

---

[6] **The state regulation of counselling and psychotherapy: sometime, never…? Richard House Magdalen Medical Practice, Lawson Road, Norwich NR3 4LF, UK**

deeper truths of the human personality that psychiatrist's mock. Depersonalisation of patients is routine in psychiatry but an anathema in psychotherapy.

Although Larkin claims that medical power is constrained and directed by governments, its power limited by a greater authority, this is not the case with psychiatry. In fact psychiatry is directive of governments, providing hypothesis to radically increase funding from government bodies. This involves the byzantine nature of psychiatric processes, its poor research methods, persuasive if fabricated claims, and the general state fear of madness and chaos.

Larkin raises the point that often doctors within the NHS are managers as much as practitioners and this again is clearer in psychiatry where the work is mainly done for them and connections to drug companies mean that psychiatrist's play a transmission or supervisory roles putting into practise the conclusions of others, agents rather than active participants. Even when researching they limit their efforts to an approved narrow range. Mainly they only diagnose, the DSM and pharmaceutical companies providing remedies again within an approved range.

Doctor and state

Doctors close association with governments means they affect political culture, doing this from an elite perspective hewing the biological hypothesis in psychiatry for example into possible forms of political intervention that could easily affect individual freedoms. If difficult people are driven only by genes with no prospect of effective psychological or moral change, then biological swamping through drugs, lifetime occupation of prisons or lifetime control by psychiatrists is the only answer. The last of these is commonly employed.

Joanna Moncrieff in *Psychiatric drug promotion and the politics of neoliberalism*[7] connects the drugs companies to the promotion of the biological hypothesis encouraging the growth of neoliberal economic and social policies: their increase is a determining factor in the 21st century.

There is a danger of elite controls of the general population being tightened with connected elite groups of social managers, politicians and doctors constructing more control through paradigms of

---

[7] The British Journal of Psychiatry. Cambridge University Press. 2018.

benevolence. Mental illness is structured around economics and the focus on work-effectively on capitalism. Will we become a hospitalised world run according to medical (an elite body) perceptions and instructions, just objects in another form of capitalist and state economic development our lives extended, fortified to medical drumbeats? Autonomous units, benevolent or not, within a national state are political units often functioning as such. While psychotherapy for example respects those they deal with, psychiatry operates outside of state laws surviving as an anomaly in liberal states.

Power

In terms of this book, medical authorities, particularly psychiatry, are authoritarian groups that exist within the paradigm of *state within a state*, functioning outside of the rules of liberal society and in doing so are constructing an authoritarian group that represents a New Right Wing, a form of fascism. It conducts itself through normalcy codes without engaging in discourse with other groups. It is also through medicine that the state itself has enlarged its areas of control, until now it rules even in the bedroom.

DARK TRIAD: Manichean, Zoroaster and Star Wars

The term The Dark Triad resembles the title of a Hammer horror film of the 1950s and 1960s but is indeed a psychiatric description of three so called personality types of an apparently distinctively nasty nature-narcissism, Machiavellian and psychopathy.[8] As often in psychiatry there appears to be a literary, indeed in this case filmic, quality and it is a surprise not to have the Wolfman suddenly appear. Dracula inhabits all three of the above so effectively he is included in everything but name. With the Dark Triad it seems reasonable to expect comic book villains to emerge bearing M, for Machiavellian, N, for Narcissist, and P for Psychopathy to jump into the room and

---

[8]

The utility of the Dark Triad model in the prediction of the self-reportedand behavioral risk-taking behaviors among adolescents. Malesza, Marta/Ostaszewski, Pawel

snarl. Or failing that, the Joker spring into life from off a DC Comics page or one of the better Bat Man films. These are of course archetypes and psychiatry holds that archetypes, principally literary techniques or used in films to hold the audience's attention and pin down the narrative, are the real measure of human beings. The subtleties of character delineation of Shakespeare, Tolstoy and D.H. Lawrence have no place in psychiatry, nor does environment reveal its many-layered head. Biological aetiology usually overwhelms all complexities of thought as a light switch takes prominence over light.

This article will concern itself with the way that psychiatry creates negative variations out of positive traits such as risk taking, an element of genius and talented artists, and why it does it. At this stage, in what will be an exploratory article, the notion is raised that psychiatry is concerned at all times with normalcy codes of mediocrity. It will also look at the symbolic nature rather than scientific nature of much psychiatric thinking and analyse why psychiatry rarely provides any genuine explanations of the disorders it identifies but simply raises a notion/image/hypothesis and then works for years to try and prove it while of course at the same employing the above to substantiate treatments.

All prisoners are bad!

The three personality traits of The Dark Triad are considered as archetypal and fixed and psychiatric papers tend only to establish the degree of fixation certain traits, in this case risk taking. Does each type take different attitudes to risk, experiencing risk differently? Now in any academic or scientific article it would be deemed necessary to define risk. What do the authors believe it is? Also, what do other scientists and academics, who consider these matters with equal professional intensity, believe. In most psychiatric papers other disciplines are routinely ignored. If a psychiatric researcher is alluding to events in history, historians are ignored, if alluding (of course) to the mind, psychology is ignored, if alluding to human culture, anthropology is ignored. Perhaps by doing so it is easier for psychiatric commentators to construct myths without fear of expert contradiction?

Why I wonder do psychiatric papers tend not to believe that comparison, synthesis and explanation are ever necessary. *A risk is a risk is a risk.* An action or series of actions preceded by states is fundamental to politics, business and cultural innovation and requires exploration, but psychiatry will have none of such wishy/washy intellectuality. Perversely, while not offering tangible proof on the actual nature of the conditions they identify, reluctant to engage in abstract examination, they take their existence as read.

First Paper

The Utility of the Dark Triad Model in the prediction of self-reported and behavioural risk-taking behaviours amongst adolescents. *Marta Malesza and Pawel Ostaszewski. Personality and Individual Differences. 90. 2016. 7-11.* These papers are referenced through a random process of selection. One psychiatric paper rarely differs from another as usually they fail to question the basic tenets of an idea or subject but merely attempt to prove it.

The first paper considered here, a worthy example of the genre (for that is what these papers are), deals with adolescents of this supposed or imagined type. The actual nature of assessments is somewhat predictive. In this instance 248 German adolescents, 109 boys and 139 girls with an age range of 14 to 18 years, were selected for the trials by their parents. In other words, parents had come to negative conclusions about their own children. The authors do not find this shocking revelation important or strange. In psychiatry, all parents likewise fit archetypes-that is kindly and responsible.

As testing and experimenting with prisoners from nearby jails apparently produces predictable results, the researchers chose adolescents instead. According to the researchers, occupants of jails fit the above stereotypes by the nature of their predicament. In their thinking it seems there is a demarcation line between normality and The Dark Triad, which appears desperately like *respectability.*' A falsely imprisoned businessman or carpenter is thereby narcissistic, Machiavellian and/or psychopathic. Such normalising and prejudiced thinking is common in the construction of this dreaded threesome. It seems not to occur to them that the part-time inhabitants of senates, parliaments and psychiatric training colleges might be better breeding grounds.

The assumption that all people in jails inhabit these states is simply childish and misinformed, demonstrating little genuine understanding of the world.[9] Indeed, it is to some extent what can be expected from relatively well-off members of a bourgeoisie viewing those less fortunate than themselves. In Victorian times the very poor stole or engaged in prostitution to survive; they were simply desperate. Many ended up in prisons, or in asylums as sufferers of the made-up category of *moral insanity*. At the same time the rich employed child prostitutes but escaped both incarceration and moral censorship. The complexities of human communities are outside the obscurantist vision of psychiatry.

Questionnaires as science

The children gathered together are given questionnaires to determine which trait they most fit, if at all. The questions seem leading with few if any variables. Two behavioural tasks, *Balloon Analog Risk Task* and *Probabilistic Discounting Task* (on a reward basis), were

---

[9] Duguid, Stephen. *Can Prisons Work? The prisoner as object and subject in modern corrections.* University of Toronto Press 2000.

also given to the young people. Each was done in laboratory conditions but without variables. The questionnaire employed is the *Adolescent Risk-Taking Questionnaire*. In addition, for good measure, the *Dirty Dozen* (no bias there) measure. Each was given randomly. Investigator effect, whereby the researcher influences results, is not anywhere considered, or does not appear to be.

Immediately the risk-taking positive and negative indicators strike the casual observer as odd. The positive is conceived of as thrill seeking and recklessness, which can present danger to others-car racing on urban streets and dangerous stunts. They provide entertainment and not much else. The negative aspects inspire similar doubts, rebelliousness and anti-socialness. While the positive traits can be viewed as anti-social according to where they lead to, rebelliousness is a largely positive trait concerned with change, challenge and intellectuality. The choices provided here appear not to be routinely subjected to analysis.

Indeed, rebelliousness as a fundamental factor of narcissism and psychopathy raises deep concerns and appears to indicate the inherent need for social control within psychiatry with a corresponding tendency to construct illnesses beyond observable realities. Our greatest minds have often been rebellious: such a list must include religious innovators such as Jesus, Muhammad and Buddha as well as eminent scientists like Einstein and Hawkings (he told off a leading astrologer when still a student). We are on dangerous ground here where normalcy is connected to obedience and submissive attitudes and indeed has the decided whiff of middle-class social ideals behind it. I dealt with this to some extent in my paper *The Intellectual History of Psychiatry*, showing that the breaking of patients mentally and reducing them to submission was evident in the early 19th century and can be seen in Kraepelin's psychiatrist declaration[10] who suggested that '*unruly individuals in dark, isolated places* (can be changed)*into gentle, submissive men and women*' through the use of the Tranquiliser Chair, which was no more than a means of torture. A commitment to Judaic forms of morality and transgression is pervasive.

Adolescent Risk Questionnaires do not normally carry indicators of The Dark Triad[11], which on a brief exploration seems connected

---

[10] One Hundred Years of Psychiatry. 1923.
[11] Gullone, Boyd, Moore. The_Adolescent_Risk-

mainly to psychiatry. Connections are made to testosterone. In my youth such individuals who favoured risk were usually assertive and athletic, not inhabiting Dark Triad territory. *The Probabilistic Discount Tasks* is itself discounted by Leonard Green and Joel Myerson[12] who have investigated claims for the process and noted a number of empirically based flaws. The test concerns impulsiveness, an apparent sign of psychopathy, etc, but the tasks seem crafted to produce pre-determined results. The authors make the point that choice is usually one dimensional in the tasks, often functioning upon time. If a choice is between two different quantities choice can be delayed and pay-off factors intervene

There are as I have noted a number of variables not employed. One is crucial to underwrite the validity of the exercise. Children and teenagers are very mischievous, often sarcastic and disruptive. Why did the researchers imagine they at any point were telling he truth or not aware of the researchers' expectations? Perhaps they were playing with the researchers. An independent variable, perhaps false

---

Taking_QuestionnaireDevelopment_and_Psychometric_Evaluation. Journal of Adolescent Research. 2000.

[12] A Discounting Framework for Choice With Delayed and Probabilistic Rewards. Psychol Bull. 2006.

questions, should have been included to check the validity of response.

Conclusions

The conclusions are interesting but predictive.

Machiavellian

Those of a Machiavellian tendency are least willing to take risks, one imagines because their calculating natures will not let them. According to the authors, Machiavellian types are only willing to take risks when there is no chance of being caught. Apart from the concentration on the negative side of risk-taking (the three types in The Dark Triad are *bad boys and girls* at all times), these are hardly risk takers if there is no risk involved. Perhaps indeed many given the chance would make excellent accountants and that placing them in the Machiavellian category demonstrated a wanton lack of imagination on the researchers' behalf. There is by the way nothing to show in any of the children's behaviour or thoughts clear evidence of Machiavellian tendencies-just the general inclinations of a questionnaire.

The tests themselves appear to carry all the weight of astrological personality tests with personality traits attached to birth signs, both self-predictive and within the realms of the tester's predicted conclusions. The suspicion is that if these tests were done on entirely random groups, they might easily produce the same outcomes. If astrological signs were added to the perspective, say 'Leos are more likely to reveal psychopathy', a similar result would certainly be obtained in order for students to prove their leadership and charismatic qualities.

The Machiavellian character was first described by the Italian Renaissance writer Machiavelli in The Prince as an instruction manual for achieving and holding onto power. It is in the tradition of medieval writers who gave advice to princes and kings on how best to rule and therefore a literary device. The text represents a break from classical philosophy and one of Machiavelli's major themes is assumed to be free will. One of the main themes of psychiatry by contrast is the control or elimination of free will. The free will dramatised by Machiavelli is one that does not exist as an active state within or outside morality, seeking instead the authentic self. This is the modern territory of Existentialist philosophers and Jungian psychologists-also, one assumes, members of The Dark Triad.

Such themes are again lost on the writers of these papers as they present people as little more than automatons reflecting the writers and researchers' intellectual scope. The thinking of Machiavelli which includes debates on morality, religion, choice, judgement and human autonomy is not on any psychiatric bookshelf. If it were no psychiatrist could possibly truly understand its purpose. Machiavelli's understanding of *virtu*[13] would leave all psychiatrists gasping for air in this rarefied atmosphere of genuine perception and intelligence. There is nothing to indicate that Machiavelli was calculating but was engaged with writing a philosophical and fictional account.

A Machiavellian type, to the extent they exist at all, analyse life for their own gain (a pointless exercise as the success of such a type

---

[13] Steiris, George. Machiavelli's Appreciation of Greek Antiquity and the Ideal of Renaissance. A. Lee, P. Peporte, H. Schnitker (eds), Renaissance? Perceptions of Continuity and Discontinuity in Europe, c.1300 - c.1550, Brill, Leiden 2010, 81-94.

such as Becky Sharpe in Vanity Fair by the British Victorian writer Thackeray, although successful in the book, is unlikely to be successful in the real world), to help others, to aid a cause, in politics, in war, in a variety of day to day interactions. It leans towards those of a driven, competitive temperament who are not bad, do not cause pervasive harm, and are not exclusively identified through power. The Machiavellian type identified in these papers calculates within the small world of individual ego. A rare type indeed, more predatory cat than human being. More likely they are represented by fun types, writers who analyse character and those who plan for profit, the very sort envied by mediocrities.

Parents putting their children forward in such an apparently cavalier way indicates abuse, but the researchers make no note of the oddity. Certainly, a somewhat strange occurrence but apart from that we have no further information on the parents and certainly not on their relationship with their own children. The researchers clearly do not believe this information is important. Thankfully though, all the social classes were represented in the surveys. What does that really mean? Were attitudes of the different classes taken, was any understanding forthcoming on relationships between child and parent? It seems not. Psychiatry does not believe that mental health problems emerge from environments: parents tend to inhabit their archetypal role and do not abuse their children in any form, representing unquestioned members of a hierarchy. All parents are responsible, caring and rarely, if ever, abuse their children.

Narcissism

According to the researchers, narcissism correlates most directly with dark personality factors, based largely it seems on the probabilistic tests. In these, the participants preferred the larger amounts that may or may not appear to the smaller amounts that will. This on one level suggests a good Stockmarket investor, although upholders of the Dark Triad would simply suggest it proves their point. Actually, it does nothing of the kind and only reveals envy on the part of the disparate authors of such papers. From other perspectives, an employee would normally commend the adolescents on their ingenuity, but the researchers relate matters from their own normalcy code.

On self-reporting processes the adolescents scored high for risk taking and anti-social preferred activities. The paper does not say whether this was simply imaginative reconstruction by the adolescents or was related to real events. As teenagers customarily envisage themselves occupied in risk-related, anti-social (a factor determined by the researchers) events described by peers or seen on television and films we cannot be sure this indicates anything other than vivid imaginations. Life and fantasy are often interwoven in teenage minds. Teenagers when self-reporting are liable to serious and playful exaggeration especially when confronted by po-faced researchers. The researchers perceive no possible gap between communication and actuality instancing perhaps extreme literal-mindedness. Nevertheless, a degree of agreement must be shown with regard to the connection between psychopathy and poor impulse control, except that the latter can simply be considered solely without the necessity to resort to the former. Where psychopathy exists at all except in extremes, it is not necessary to ascribe undeveloped issues of control with extremes of personality mainly understood as a one-dimensional archetype.

Narcissism is described as connected to those who are over optimistic and exaggerate their abilities. Again, while no doubt there are many examples in the world, there is again a certain theatrical, histrionic quality to the descriptions with inklings of moral values attached. Narcissism is something of a curiosity as it always requires an observer. The individual claiming to be a great tennis player might actually be one just not known as such to the observer who may know nothing of tennis. As much else with psychiatry, it depends largely on the psychiatrist's prejudices as to whether or not someone is narcissistic or genuinely talented. Conversely, no one accuses the psychiatrist of narcissism for believing he or she understands others, something few people are capable of. Psychiatrist arrogance is surely a hint at narcissistic personality traits.

Psychopathy, attached to many normative traits of boredom and frustration, also has an approach to risks, which takes them over it seems. Whether people not belonging to the Dark Triad suffer similarly when faced with negative states of mind is rarely accessed for if they do, they are immediately assigned in a no-win situation to

The Dark Triad. Although random tests are performed, they express the validity-problems identified here. With a number of my clients I certainly noticed many parents that met the conditions of the above personality types, but none were identified as such.

2.

Papers on the Dark Triad identify many as cruel and callous but that can easily be seen as simply part of human nature, and one noticeable in psychiatrists as well as others. If psychiatrists exhibit Dark Triad qualities, is it not possible that the manipulative traits proposed within Dark Triad archetypes indicate that psychiatry was constructed to provide doctors with vast salaries and status?

Here as elsewhere human traits are introduced into psychiatric normalcy codes, defined and established by the profession and not actually necessarily true. Behaviour is predicted and moral value judgements, which psychiatrists should not be making, are clumsily attached. The questionnaires again predict certain triats, always negative ones, but not the positive traits a more positive commentator would note. They appear self-fulfilling. The scientific nature is highly dubious. Were the participants asked for their permission before the tests began, or just their parents? Were the parents similarly tested as well as the investigators? Again, were any checks made on the veracity of the adolescent's answers or were their responses just assumed to be genuine? The biases demonstrated towards prisoners shows narrow unthinking approaches to the world in general but also the avoidance of individual narratives by psychiatry. What appears the case is that a whole range of human thoughts, actions and intentions are negatively packaged up within comic book archetypes. Although there are a number of very dangerous people in the world, the individualistic truly dangerous ones are few and warrant individual approaches not the one shoe, or three shoes, approach here.

The Dirty Dozen

The comic book nature of the general thinking is evident here perhaps or is this just an instance of the irresponsible personality type of those of the Dark Triad. *"We seek him here, we seek him there, we seek the Dark Triad everywhere.*"[14] Here, this paper will review self-reporting questionnaires of the above.

1. I tend to seek prestige and status.

    Surely the compilers of the test are doing the same as is everyone who puts their name to any academic paper or creative work. To consider this part of a dark personality is ludicrous. (Narcissistic)

2. I tend to want everyone to admire me.

    Is this not the trait of every high-achieving athlete, scientist (including Einstein), writer and politician (although here they might have a point). Is every high-achiever a member of the Dark Side? (Narcissistic)

3. I tend to be callous or insensitive.

---

[14] *The Scarlet Pimpernel.* Baroness Emmuska Orczy, 1905.

Individuals can act this way for a number of reasons and as these questions are not qualified such questions demonstrate nothing. People are prone to answer tests for a variety of reasons. The need to impress. The need to express a self-truth. *Psychopathy.*

4. I tend to manipulate others to get my way.

    Before intelligent and beautiful women were allowed to fashion careers, many acted like this at some kind or another. The trait was environmental not inherent. Also, many teenagers, just discovering their sexuality, like to think they have power over others, but rarely do. (Machiavellian)

The questions do not get any more coherent. Surely, such tests resemble the personality tests in Sunday magazines. Answering honestly to any or all of these questions could get you labelled and locked up by the local psychiatrist, so ridiculous is this manufactured premise.

To what extent are these moral testaments employed by psychiatry in order to widen its scope and thereby pathologize criminality, taking it away from law courts and into their own embrace? The criminal mind might simply be different, examples of areas of human society that are not domesticated. Is psychiatry, with its desire for submission and obedience, merely part of the ongoing process of human domestication? A further definition is available.

A person who cares about others, who is empathetic, and moral, would be impotent to achieve his/her egoistic goals. [15] While this is interesting it appears politically based and has little to do with human psychology as such, and much to do with how we view those opposed to our viewpoint. This is a description of someone not of the dark side-the similarity to Star Wars is tempting-the member of the Dark Side or Dark Triad is high utilitarianism, practical and goal orientated, and low empathy. The idea of the Dark Triad gained in popularity from the time of the earliest Star Wars films and strangely

---

[15] . Czarna, Jonason, Dufner, Kossowska.*The Dirty Dozen Scale: Validation of a Polish Version and extension of the Nomological Net*. Frontiers in Psychology. 2016. Page 6.

seems to reflect the Dark Side premise of two human groups inhabiting opposed moral and personality spectrums. Both these groups, according to psychiatry, are engaged in eternal warfare with psychiatry to the fore waving light sabres of medication. Actually, this is the Manichean viewpoint resuscitated into the present-the product of Zoroaster in which *Ahura Mazda*, the god of light and fire, is engaged in perpetual warfare with *Arhiman*, the god of darkness. Is the Dark Triad merely then a psychiatric metaphor for people they fear or simply do not like or understand? Where is psychiatry within this metaphor, among the wielders of Light Sabres or members of the Dark Side, the propagators of empire? Psychiatry objectifies people, has practised lobotomies and ECT on vulnerable groups, seeks both power and status, represent what is largely a pseudo-science, its individual members holding themselves to be more intelligent and important than they actually are, insist on submission and obedience from those they deal with and assume an alarming indifference to human rights. So, where exactly? Is it not the case that those perpetuating these myths themselves already inhabit The Dark Side?

The inclusion of *moral* in the above quote does not embrace its fluidity or cultural differences. The morals are based on Christian beliefs, and the writer of every paper on The Dark Triad seems unable to comprehend the aetiology of their concepts of goodness and morality. None appear to have read Nietzsche or the Existentialists but as they are concerned with science (sic) and the above theorists' philosophy, why should they? Commonplace notions are accepted because abstract thinking is too difficult? While they employ terms such as morality and goodness it is not necessary that they should understand them also.

The Dark Triad seems religious in scope, not scientific. The Triad are little more than members of a destructive pantheon common in ancient religion, expressing also the demons of medieval times. Intellectually, the Dark Triad is a backward step. People who act destructively are no longer wounded by poor family environments or survivors from terrible conditions and war but are born bad. [16] *This is neo-conservatist reactionism within a psychological framework reflecting psychiatric values.*

---

[16] Jacobwitz/Sharon, Egan, Vincent. *The Dark Triad and Normal Personality Traits.* Personality and Individual Differences. 2006.

While we all accept the nature of goodness within the above descriptions placing them together merely creates an idealistic framework: human personality is made up of several traits that emerge and wilt according to the environment. The rise of neo-conservative and reactionary thinking in psychiatry cannot hide this. The liberal psychiatric tropes based on debate and discussion have faded before psychiatric certainty and autocracy.

The values the commentators on the Dark Triad express community values, packaged as normality, and this should be regarded with suspicion. In the past, and still in many countries, morality remains the province of religion; here they are the province of psychiatry and as such lead away from not towards understanding. Within psychiatry these are merely packages of traits bundled together. An additional issue is that these 'goodness' or 'normality' values are Christian values representing cultural not universal determinants. There is no understanding evident in any of a dozen papers read but each appears to be claiming the discovery of goodness for psychiatry. Not only are these community and Christian values but ones determined by centuries of ethical thinkers. Again, the producers of these papers exhibit no awareness of the intellectual background and sheer effort involved. *The expression of goodness, citizenship, conservatism, obedience and ultimately submission underlying the ideas of The Dark Triad is comparable to right wing or reactionary thinking but without the subtlety of great Far Right thinkers. In this thinking, you are born evil-just like the demons hiding under your bed. This represents the triumph of mediocrity.*

Laboratory Psychiatry

My paper *The Intellectual History of Psychiatry* categorises modern psychiatry as *Laboratory Psychiatry*. Psychiatry determines the nature of mental illness through laboratory experiments on rodents and employs as here laboratory tests-questionnaires and computer based Probabilistic tests-to determine personality traits. It never employs natural experiments but only engages in experiments it can control. The contrary nature of questionnaires seems unknown to them as also the commonly referenced ethics concerning participants' rights. Results seem not to be further qualified but taken as literal expressions of past and future acts. The result is not reality, the complexities of human nature and life, but a reconstructed reality that conforms to their prejudices and desire for power and status.

Philip Zimbardo's 1973 prison experiment alongside his 2007 text *The Lucifer Effect: How good people turn evil*, Stanley Milgram's simulated torture experiments in the early 1960s, Asch's procedures (1950s) present genuine scientific research (of a kind) into the nature of evil and should be consulted alongside this myth-making approach. Hannah Arendt has produced volumes on the destructive nature of human beings. I wonder if this is the very best psychiatry can offer: comic book psychology.

Psychiatry and Eugenics: the White Man's Science

The problem of ethnic degeneration concerned early European psychiatrists of the 19th century and drove somatic investigation into the brain, coupled with concerns with eugenics. Purifying the human population of its dangerous racial defects emerged of course in full bloodied fury within Nazism of the following century. This paper must be viewed alongside *John Locke, Slavery and Psychology* involving the theme of Western colonisation from the 17th century until the middle of the 20th century as the drive behind the psychological sciences.

At this time eugenic investigations interested medical doctors, biological scientists and social scientists. Many, including famous intellectuals such as H.G. Wells whose *War of the Worlds* is about the cleansing of the world of human beings, were drawn to the idea.

Psychiatrists were particularly interested in eugenic ideas with regard to diagnosis and treatment.[17] Eugenics had many roots but certainly one, particularly in the USA, involved racism, racial purity and the breeding of racial elites. The idea of improving the *White Races* prevailed. Racism was the dirty secret, both ignored and recognised, of 19th century and early 20th century European and American societies and *sciences*.

Frank W. Stahnisch (2014)[18] introduces many intellectual precedents such as Alfred Ploetz (1860/1940), Margaret Sanger (1879-1966) who's drive towards contraception involved controlling populations, preventing perhaps bad blood infecting it. While this involved degenerate genes-those who had been in prison-behind it also lay the fear of infection by black or non-white genes and madness. Degenerate genes, especially of the insane, were by then considered genetic defects thought to pass down through families, evidenced in

---

[17] Stahnisch, Frank W. *The Early Eugenics Movement and Emerging Professional Psychiatry: Conceptual Transfers and Professional Relationships between Germany and North America, 1880s to 1930s.* Canadian Bulletin of medical history. 2014.
[18] Stahnisch, Frank W. *The Early Eugenics Movement and Emerging Professional Psychiatry: Conceptual Transfers and Professional Relationships between Germany and North America, 1880s to 1930s.* Canadian Bulletin of medical history. 2014.

the stories of Edgar Allen Poe, particularly *The Fall of the House of Usher*. The introduction of degenerative *blood* or genes was ambiguously investigated in the Bronte sister's novels *Jane Eyre*, where the mad mixed-race wife in the attic suffers from two alleged defects, and *Wuthering Heights*.

Jane Eyre[19]

Charlotte Bronte's *Jane Eyre* is the narrative of a young woman seeking to create her own way in life, thereby having some connection to Thackeray's *Vanity Fair,* both published in 1948.[20] Jane Eyre is a scrupulous version of Becky Sharpe who employs her sexual charms to make a fortune. Jane Eyre unfortunately is plain and habitually claims to act with autonomous honesty and good character. They represent opposing notions of virtue and ambition. Jane meets Mr Rochester, her future husband, working in his household as a governess. Although he proposes to her, she shortly afterwards discovers he is already married to Bertha Antoinette Mason, a Creole woman locked up in the attic and described as a

---

[19] Mckee, Patricia. *Racial Strategies in Jane Eyre.* Cambridge University Press. 2009. Online 2009.

[20] http://www.quarterly-review.org/classic-qr-the-original-1848-review-of-jane-eyre/18-11-2019

lunatic. It appears that Rochester married Bertha for her money and brought her to England only to lock her up. The text is ambiguous. Although Jane is portrayed as virtuous, she also aids the marginalisation of a black woman, perceiving Rochester as a victim rather than a rogue. In many ways this is a tract on colonialism, whether the author intended this or not, and reflects the nature of Britain's 19th century wealth based on the slave trade. Like black people in America Bertha is deprived of her liberty and made into the sexually voracious *Other*.

That Jane Eyre refers to Mr Rochester as *her master* adds additional ambiguity to the text and extends the notion of slavery (see my *A History of Slavery*) as in other circumstances Bertha, Rochester's wife, could be *his* slave. Bertha's burning down Rochester's house at the end of the novel extends the idea of blood-corruption, this act alone the direct consequence of the threat of shared ethnic genes. Other signs of symbolism in the novel are the name of Rochester's home, Thornfield, indicating a place of trouble and pain, and his fiancé upon meeting Jane, Blanche (white) Ingram who looks down on Jane as her inferior and is exposed in the novel as mercenary.

In 1966 *Wide Sargasso Sea* [21] Jean Rhys wrote a counterblast to Bronte's Jane Eyre telling the narrative from Bertha's perspective whereby her blackness and mental instability are inseparable, her madness constructed by the colonialist Rochester. In Rhys' novel Bertha is the name given to her by her husband. Her real name is Antoinette Cosway. Her actual name indicates her possible racial but certainly foreign background. She is locked up because she is black and potentially mad, not perhaps because she is mentally unstable. By changing her name, Mr Rochester changed her identity and here the narrative can refer to Victorian patriarchy and the way husbands hid unwanted wives in asylums and can equally reference the way people's identities are removed today and restructured by psychiatry with often implausible descriptive diagnosis. The colonialist treatise works both in *Jane Eyre* and *Wide Sargasso Sea* as in the former it depicts how black people were dispossessed of land and their freedom, while in the later it shows how the mad, or those marginalised as such, are dispossessed of their identity and subject to

---

[21] Kamel, Rose. "Before I was set Free: The Creole Wife in "Jane Eyre" and the "Wide Sargasso Sea". *The Journal of Narrative Technique* Vol. 25, No. 1 (Winter, 1995), pp. 1-22

incarceration. In each instance a dominant authoritarian group decides on the nature of identity.

Emily Bronte's Wuthering Heights produces a similar interpretation, where Heathcliff can be viewed through a racial and racialist spectrum[22]. Although described as resembling a gypsy, it is just as likely he is mixed race.[23] Although Heathcliff is seen as *'maddened'* because of his treatment (like black people in America and elsewhere) he is also described as primal, a creature of emotion and temper, like Berthe, bringing corruption and wildness into civilised (sic) British society. In effect the British can equally be seen as colonising opportunists who have robbed Berthe of her inheritance and Heathcliff of his self-respect. They are feared as likely to corrupt British bloodlines, White racial purity, and therefore must be marginalised and hidden away. In both cases, the madness lies not with the black characters, Heathcliff and Berthe, but with the hidden knowledge of slavery as the basis for family wealth. The

---

[22] Kreilkamp, Ivan. **Petted Things: Wuthering Heights and the Animal** The Yale Journal of Criticism
Johns Hopkins University Press Volume 18, Number 1, Spring 2005 . pp. 87-110
10.1353/yale.2005.0006

[23] Von Sneidern, Maja-Lisa, Wuthering Heights and the Liverpool Slave Trade.
ELH. Vol 62 No 1 Cambridge University Press.1995.

degeneration of Hindley Earnshaw and the effete character of Edgar Linton in Wuthering Heights are symbolic of the threat to Anglo-Saxon bloodlines by the black or dark Other-Heathcliff, a life force, is the incoming corruption. Both Thornfield and Wuthering Heights represent traditional British society of the period, and both are in one way or another destroyed by the Other, Bertha and Heathcliff, members of *degenerate* ethnic groups.

Here strides psychiatry

Although the writer itemises Germany and the USA, equally they could have identified the UK as prominent in the development of Eugenics. Nevertheless, they focus on a group of German intellectuals and doctors who came together under the group name *The Pacific*. These included Ploetz, Ferdinand Simon (1861-1912), Carl Hauptmann, the physiologist Gustav von Bunge (1844-1920) and the anthropologist Rudolf Poech (1870-1921), who joined up with the brain psychiatrist Auguste Forel (1848-1931). Forel called for the sterilisation of the of the mentally ill for the sake of the nation. Only *'quality people'* deserved to live. They of course, privileged, white, and educated decided who were quality and who were not, which boiled down to middleclass people very similar to themselves-not that far away from psychiatry. Forel although famous by his own efforts at the time was a follower of Francis Galton who, inspired by Charles Darwin, developed the science of Eugenics.[24] Several connections between Eugenics, its desire for the quantitative and qualitative improvement of humankind and its authoritarian, right wing[25] bias, and psychiatry can perhaps be found here. Psychiatric treatment is driven onto patients, forced, with a passion reminiscent of Early Modern Christianity's determination to purify nations of sin-it indeed in its approach resembles eugenicist's desire for ethnic hygiene. The clarifying of every action and emotional state within psychiatric descriptivism demonstrates the same obsessive, opportunistic zeal.

Ploetz and his wife subsequently emigrated to the USA becoming involved in concerns there on human breeding and the creation of better US citizens. Ploetz became involved with American Eugenicists in American universities, while shortly after developing

---

[24] Galton, G.J, and C. J. Francis Galton: And Eugenics Today. Journal of Medical Ethics. Vol. 24. No. 2 2019.
[25] This term is employed with reluctance but nevertheless reflects many of psychiatry's questionable beliefs.

his own research into heredity, or what we now call genetics. The biological assumptions of the aetiology of mental illness is no more than ancient hereditary/madness/bad blood repackaged.

The authors point out that as well as concerns with hygiene and human sanitation that eugenics was also rooted in, he and his fellow travellers tended to be *Nordic Supremacists*. Later, with the American Eugenicist, Davenport, Ploetz developed racist notions of race competition, essentially of racial hygien. The White or Nordic race had to ensure its purity in order to remain the dominant race.[26]

Psychiatry and Eugenics

The term Racial Hygiene, with its essential logic based on Francis Galton's ideas, was accepted in one way or another by leading psychiatrists of the early 20th century such as Emile Kraepelin (1856-1926) often considered the first genuine psychiatrist, and Robert Sommer (1864-1937). Forel and Kraepelin believed that mental illness was hereditary and thereby mad lines needed to be cleaned up.[27] Many German physicians were led by Pasteur's

---

[26] Lewis, Ricki. *White Supremacy-the Dark Side of Eugenics.* MedicalXPress. 2017.
[27] Weindling, Paul. Psychiatry and the Holocaust. Psychological Medicine. Vol.22. Issue 1. 1992

advances to believe that the germs of mental illness could be similarly found and eradicated. Some physicians believed that therapy for the insane was wrong as it merely kept them alive and the State's needs had to come before the rights of individuals, a position explored in the modern world by Gerald Roche[28]in a PhD paper concerning laws used to incarcerate the mentally ill and the occurrence of wrongful imprisonment and state authoritarianism based on the word alone of psychiatrists.

Led in that direction by some of Galton's earlier ideas, the *Racial Hygienists* began to discuss how to achieve their aims through considered forms of treatment. Behavioural correction was one idea, specifically in mental hospitals. A repeat of moral treatment in effect in earlier madhouses-forcing people to act sane rather than be sane. Ploetz encouraged the idea that greater concern with heredity, or gene therapy, would help eugenicists and psychiatrists create the best German stock as it increased again after the First World War.

[28] A philosophical investigation into coercive psychiatric practices

2 Volumes
8wekyb3d8bbwe/TempState/Downloads/A_philosophical_investigation_into_co
erc%20(1).pdf

Although biological determinism, the main focus of psychiatry since the 1950s, seems to be based on *Racial Hygienist* ideas, the genesis of *The Dark Triad* hypothesis roots some of its ideas in extreme right wing thinking as seen in the belief in the conjunction between human hereditary and badness.

Organic versions of statehood lay behind the beliefs of the eugenicists, thereby as a human body degenerates so can the nation or ethnic group (Stahnisch. 2014). In this paper its infection is from other ethnic groups that threaten White ethnicity. Treatment of the mentally ill, where it was applied, thereby functioned as the medical policing of degeneracy, surreptitiously racial. The role of psychiatry was thereby to protect the state from degenerate genes that resulted from colonial paradigms. Although the nature of that mission has subtly changed, their role remains vigilance over degenerate genes and attempts to suppress their spread. One crucial and evident role of modern psychiatry remains the identification of *mad* ideas and behaviour and of removing the perpetrators from the body politic. Prior to the First World War it was common for German psychiatrists to consider that cultural degeneracy had spread and with it the potency of the nation.

This paper holds that the degeneracy noted by European and American psychiatrists had a colonial base and was enforced by a fear of other races. The purification of genes continues today but now has its own volition. Stahnisch (2014:26) perceives the psychiatric search for morphological alterations in the human brain due to degeneracy to have continued after the First World War and developed into cultural and social currency that expanded in Germany after its defeat in 1918 and has thereby seeped into Psychiatry's worldview.

Psychiatry, Power, Universal Ideologies and the Nazis

Two previous papers should be considered at length alongside this specific effort-*An Unusual Power: The Cultural Construction of Madness*, which in its final pages deals with the issue of domestication and mental health ideologies, and *Psychiatry and*

Eugenics: the White Man's Science, twinned as the discerning might see. This paper relies on the two above and is also a continuation of both, particularly the latter insisting that the biological approach by psychiatry meets the needs of self-domestication.

Self-domestication

Ideas found in 1930s biological estimates of race and personality still linger in modern discourse and understandings of human nature and can equally be seen in an early hypothesis constructed upon human domestication at the onset of agriculture several thousand years ago.[29] Charles Darwin realised that domesticated animals were very different from wild ones, possessing distinguishable traits that wild animals did not possess. This he called *'the domestication syndrome'* since many commentators concentrated on traits rather than genetic

---

[29] Brune, Martin. *On human self-domestication, psychiatry and eugenics.* Philosophy, ethics and humanities in medicine. Link.springer.com/article/10.1186/1747-5341-2-21* 2007.

causes. Adam S. Wilkins et al[30] believe the syndrome results from mild changes in the embryo's neural crest cell. This changed the wild animal involving increased docility and tameness and according to the writers physical changes and alterations in adrenocorticotropic hormone levels and the concentration of some neurotransmitters, prolonging juvenile behaviour, changing brain size and regions. There are other beliefs but they will not necessarily be recounted here. Darwin published his conclusions a few years after Gregor Mendel (1822-1884) published his inheritance ideas.

Self-domestication, psychiatrists alleged, explained the degeneration of human genes that produced mental illness. It is a hierarchical proposition examining changes from better to worse, and offered a specific psychiatric ideology. Also, this encouraged the dissemination of Social Darwinist ideas of avoiding procreation with lower genetic human value translated as differences in colour, culture, and in mental health-the last concerning differences in thinking and behaviour that by and large could not be fitted into

---

[30] The Domestication Syndrome in Mammals: A Unified Explanation Based on Neural Crest Cell Behavior and Genetics. GENETICS 2014.

normalcy codes. The process includes the transmission of the imagined lower genetic values[31].

Brune (2007) believes that biological psychiatry early became the ideology of choice as domestication suggested human kind could change or adjust itself, and that this in effect could be speeded up by medical, that is psychiatric, assistance. Its height, he suggests, was during the Nazi period in Germany where the ruling elite sought to create a pure race by exterminating inferior types. Does psychiatry seek to improve humans by eliminating faults such as depression and anxiety rather than understand why they are there and accept them? Perhaps anxiety is not a lower human genetic value that prevents people working at times or expressing constant positive values but a necessary rejoinder to a world factored on work?

Self-domestication involves physical and supposedly biological changes in human beings as the result of turning towards faming and ceasing to be hunter-gatherers. People became shorter, less powerful and died younger but as the result of our sedentary lifestyle

---

[31] *Psychiatry and Eugenics: the White Man's Science*

gradually there were more of us and cereal crops and livestock made a more secure food source for more people. In order for aurochs, giant ancestors of modern cattle, to be controlled they were bred to be smaller-the larger bulls were weeded out, and effectively cattle shrank. They bred out aggression where they could. They did the same with sheep, goats and pigs-bred from boars. Animals were bred therefore to be docile, to live in pens and killed at will.

The theory goes that human beings were made more docile in order to more easily reside together in large settlements and eventually cities. Hierarchies were formed and religion appeared as a central point for early communities. Each of these social and ideological factors may have changed human nature and even biology. Within the above hierarchies is a greater tendency towards conformity and therefore greater support for entrenched political systems. Every known political system is backed-up by advances to or away from religious intensity and often in line with the power of priests. Religion and democracy for example may not be good bedfellows.

Domestication also means the understanding of civilisation and civilised behaviour as external and internal control of individuals. For some two hundred years, psychiatry, an elite group belonging mainly to the upper regions of the middle class, have independently framed mental health within conformist and moral paradigms structured upon their own autocratic behaviour. In the 1930s and 1940s for example, in line with the racism and violence within Europe, psychiatrists lobotomised lesbians and transgender individuals under the general label of perversion as a mental illness. Throughout psychiatry the real or imagine promiscuity of others was restructured as moral madness for example. These were assumed from the Judaic religions. Commonly people who were different (a process continued to the present) would sometimes suffer enforced invasive treatments of drugs or electric shocks that affected their individuality.

The legitimate nature of homosexuality became a power battle between homosexual groups and psychiatry, which held that same-sex sexual activity, was a disorder, holding like monotheistic priests that sex and procreation were indissolubly connected.[32] Apart from many other issues, such as doubtful involvement in morality and instituting thereby confusion with medicine, its cultural rather than universal roots, and its enormous power for psychiatry or psychiatrists could order homosexuals into treatment, it raises serious questions about psychiatry's legitimacy. In the 1930s and 1940s non-conformist sexual behaviour was dealt with a range of invasive treatments, such as lobotomy. Modern models of treatment, *drugs*, can extinguish individuality, thinking and initiative thereby leading to greater hegemony or at least greater conformity. Psychiatric drugs create docile, obedient citizens. The policing role of psychiatry is in line with governmental concerns with order.

Interestingly, it is almost impossible to find in official psychiatric papers work done on psychiatric abuse even in the distant past, although there have been an immense number of books, including by esteemed medical historians, on the subject. Psychiatry remains completely, or almost completely, mute on its many instances of abuse. The terrible events within 1930s-1950s psychiatry did not happen, although everyone knows it did. Again interestingly,

---

[32] Bayer, Ronald. Homosexuality and American Psychiatry: The Politics of Diagnosis. Princeton University Press. 1987.

psychiatrists write papers on Russian Communist psychiatric abuse of dissidents but not about their own treatment of outspoken individuals. Many commentators believe psychiatric abuse in the past was a thing of evil, but suppose it still goes on?

The placing of homosexuality and lesbianism into diagnostic parameters meant they were ill, diseased, and subject to enforced treatment. It is not widely known, but doctors can still enforce treatment no matter if that treatment is the best or worst on offer. For many years all means of treatments were tried. The early psychiatrist Paul Moreau considered homosexuality as a congenital weakness, a perversion and hereditary trait due to bad habits such as masturbation. Ideas of free will, of legitimacy of choice, did not then as they rarely do now occur to psychiatrists. Conformity to middle class morality was then as now the key to normality. Thirty years ago psychiatrists decided deep religious belief was a form of mental illness, in the present environment they do not and cannot do so. Is mental illness a movable feast indulged in by psychiatrists? Alan Turing, one of the greatest minds of his generation, committed suicide probably as a direct result of psychiatric treatment to cure his homosexuality. Ronald Bayer (1987) considers psychiatric involvement in the political construction of homosexuality as constructive, as in 1970 they took it off their list of diseases thereby further legitimising it, but why was it on there in the first place and what exactly had it to do with the profession? Although I have spent immense time on homosexuality as an example of psychiatric prejudices, religious and creative people also fell and fall foul of psychiatry.

Present societies

Present western society consists of groups in which the individual units recognise each other through political or fashion perspectives or are aligned against other groups fashion or political perspective, through territory, education, wealth and poverty. Individual is expressed within paradigms of conformity. There are no genuine overlords, just rule by those who gain most through their position in one group or another.

German racism

Growing European racism was aided by psychiatry based on the above ideas of self-domestication, seen as necessary while also providing evidence of degeneracy. Concerned with genetic heredity it was effectively the first universal biological approach. In Germany this was complicated by another system of ideas that harked back to a more vital past referencing Aryan (more to do with Persians) warriors and conquerors before the influx of inferior genes from African slavery, colonialism and the Near East (largely Jews).[33] This affected many other European countries, although it was not solely a white man's delusion. In *Psychiatry and Eugenics: the White Man's Science* I detailed at length the connection between Early Modern psychiatry colonialism, racism and eugenics.

Brune (2007) highlights the goal orientated process of research and experiments with animals, changing them to assist human needs. Rodents are being domesticated in laboratories to provide evidence for the efficacy of drugs which are then employed on human beings. The belief that by doing so there is some correspondence with the latter is probably a logical fallacy and the information found may

---

[33] Psychiatry and Eugenics: The White Man's Science.

simply be based on need over actuality. Although drugs for depression are developed in this fashion, the results may be manipulated by the above and regurgitated in object related fantasy. Persuading patients of their efficacy makes up their very efficacy.[34] The researchers' goal becomes the actuality no matter what issues arise to undermine such a view. The psychiatrist's gaze is fixed on their own power, theories and solutions not the object-the patient. Whereas genuine science concerns subject-object, psychiatry concerns *itself*, its practices and power, when viewing the nature of the object, thereby reiterating reflective knowledge.

Mental illness, eugenics, psychiatry and racism

Amir Teicher references a decision faced by the anthropologist Otto on the marriage of his daughter to a man whose family were tainted with mental illness, and whether their children would suffer from the same problem. Heredity factors of mental illness were commonly believed then, often tied up with racist concepts. Examining the

---

[34] Conformity paradigms here must be noted. Stanley Milgam's and Zimbardo's Stanford Prison Experiment, although now appropriately criticised demonstrate individual and group conformity.

letters between the two scientists, Teicher explores how social and cultural difference was transformed into racial or biological difference. [35] Reche was an important scientist and member of the Nazi party who helped form prevailing ideologies of race and racial inferiority. Rudin was of a similar intellectual background but in his work on psychiatric genetics has had a considerable effect on modern psychiatry.

At this stage, eugenics and the theory of the transference of diseased or malformed genes were locked into psychiatric determinism. Many psychiatrists were eugenicists. The policy that began in the USA of sterilisation of the weak minded had reached Germany during the post-war Weimer government and of course was fiercely appropriated under the Nazi regime. Purity of the gene pool was the main concern, eradicating difference from Western white hegemony.

Reche's concerned approach was just one of many that reached the German Institute of Psychiatry in Munich headed by Rudin from 1931. Of consequence is that Reche's concerns on medical hygiene

[35]Teicher, Amir. Father of the Bride and the Biologization of Social Animosity in Nazi Germany, 1937-1941.
https://www.academia.edu/41339999/Father_of_the_Bride_or_the_Biologizatio n_of_Social_Animosity_in_Nazi_Germany

were paralleled by those on race. For Reche the health of the individual, posed as genetic paradigm of latent illness, was expressed in line with national and ethnic health. The two were inseparable. This understanding of the genetic latency of mental illness was also accompanied by the German Supreme Court's understanding of its disease components. Racial impurity for example was contagious. Mental illness was and still is considered an impurity.

If the racial laws of the USA, particularly Virginia,[36] and Germany during the same historical period are considered, the same process is noted between diseases, and mental illness and race in that it is both biological and transmitted. The genes that carry racial impurities are subject to professional investigation and definition. A white person with black grandparents would effectively be black as the impure genes outweigh the pure genes, indicating that pure genes are weak and needed protection, as anyone with mentally ill grandparents would be potentially mentally ill and genetically impure. In each

---

[36] Scales-trent, Judy. Racial purity laws in the United States and Nazi Germany; the targeting process. Human Rights Quarterly. The johns Hopkins university press. 2001.

case the authorities of purity and impurity are pure, and in both instances members of the medical or psychiatric professions. In both instances they feel threatened by those impurities and the loss of personal and group identity. *A psychiatrist for example places himself on the side of normality, or purity, in control of and policing impurities as designated by psychiatry.*

Genes nevertheless are not pure or impure but are designated as such according to social valuation. In psychiatry impurity, mental difference or illness, is specified in the same or similar way to the German psychiatrists above who were concerned with both racial and mental impurities and the racial purists of Virginia. Both groups believe genes can be impure and require policing and weeding out. The latter stage concerns eugenics, in that the impure genes need expelling or excising. The perceived standard is arrived at by groups who because of race, wealth and entitlement hold themselves to be pure deciding on the impurities of others.

Ernst Rudin

Rudin was a celebrated psychiatrist who became a fervent Nazi. Born in Switzerland his brother in law was Alfred Ploetz, who has been met before in *Psychiatry and Eugenics: the White Man's Science.* Ploetz developed ideas on racial hygiene and Social Darwinism in Germany after 1890. He also worked in Emile Kraepelin's lab, another believer in right wing ideas and eugenics. There Rudin developed his idea of *'empirical genetic prognosis'*. From 1917 until 1945 he was the director of the Genealogical-Demographic Department at the German Institute for Psychiatric Research. Rudin believed that mental illnesses were caused by recessive genes, although not quite the same as modern psychiatry which instead believes in malfunctioning genes and neurons which involves little interaction with society. After 1933, the National Socialist Party (Nazi) endorsed his work. The Rockefeller Foundation, already met as an encourager of lobotomy[37], was also a funder. As Matthias Weber says the Nazi health policy needed a scientific theory for its actions. These involved eugenics and the later extermination of Jews, homosexuals, gypsies, mentally ill and others with diseased genes. [38]

---

[37] *An Unusual Power: Fabrication and Funding. Psychiatry's Early 20th Century Renaissance.*

[38] Weber, Matthias M. *Ernst Rubin, 1874-1952: A German psychiatrist and geneticist.* American Journal of Medical Genetics. 1996.

Rael D. Strous[39] writes that doctors, particularly geneticists of the period and psychiatrists, played a central role in Nazi crimes. While this is well known, less well known is the thought processes behind their excesses remain equally central to modern psychiatry. Leonard Conti, the Reich's chief physician, had proudly declared that physicians had been amongst the first Nazi. In *Psychiatry and Eugenics: the White Man's Science* I have detailed how psychiatrists created the earliest racist and eugenic organisations. Before 1933 and Hitler's acquisition of power, 3000 doctors were already Party members. 38000 had joined by 1942, it seems willingly.

Eugenics and psychiatry

The differences considered in psychiatry are ultimately social ones. Inferior social positions mean an inferior person, restructured by psychiatry as mentally ill. The epitome of human purity is class based. Social conservatism, powerfully seen in *The Dark Triad*, is an equal barometer of mental stability or mental impurities and is a

---

[39] *Hitler's Psychiatrists: Healers and Researchers Turned Executioners and its Relevance Today.* Ethics. 2009.

vigorously conservative or right wing construct that mirrors the heredity biological basis of Rudin's ideas. In 1930s-to 1950s the use of lobotomy for a wide range of real and imagined medical problems destroyed the individual as a means of destroying impurities. Patients became unchallenging and obedient; in effect it was eugenics with a still living victim. Now as then defining the impurities is a one way process involving psychiatric determinism. Mental illness as a complex situational prospect does not actually exist in modern psychiatry now or in the past-our way or the bye way. Discourse between psychiatry and patient remains non-existent and still resembles the two processes exampled above.

Nazi Germany, the Holocaust and Psychiatry

Psychiatry was at the forefront in Nazi Germany's eugenics and racist agenda, partly as the consequence of the returnees from the USA. Nevertheless, right wing politics and psychiatry seem to have merged from the period following the 1st world war. Even today, much of the vocabulary of psychiatric writings bears the stamp of right wing states of mind. During the Nazi period in Germany almost

300,000 mentally ill patients were murdered under the Mendelian belief that they had inherited their illnesses. This was at a time when enforced sterilisation of patients was being conducted in Western countries, led by Rudin in Germany. [40] Although there was a rapid increase in mental illness in Europe and USA this was on the heels of the Great Depression. Strous (2009) warns doctors not to let this happen again, but perhaps it is through drugs and the unusual power bestowed on doctors themselves. Rudin, with his eager colleagues, created the processes for the annihilation of the mentally ill in Germany but also the means for the extermination of many others.

A universal concept of biological determinism has placed enormous power in the hands of psychiatry yet again, and such power is related or can be related to recognisable political outcomes. The Dark Triad is one socially divisive form, will there be others?

---

[40] Torrey and Yolken. *Psychiatric Genocide: Nazi Attempts to Eradicate Schizophrenia*. Schizophrenia Bulletin. 2010.

Criminology, Psychopathology, Dehumanisation, and Morlocks

"The Anatomy of Violence"

Psychiatry functions within a set of beliefs that often have a tenuous relationship to the world in general. The crucial determinants of psychopathology rest on a social and historical concept that owes everything to a specific set of perceptions. The scientific validity of that viewpoint is unproven and is of a kind that would naturally resist proof. Connected to the biological approach, sprung out the hypotheses of Richard Dawkins extrapolated on in *The Selfish Gene*, it is a widely held contextual concept of modern psychiatry. This biological view concerns a specific view of society focusing on certain members of society who clearly belong to a separate form of humanity, a lower class and are most seen amongst the underprivileged. Biological psychiatry employs a dehumanising metamorphosis to achieve its aims. It also involves a specific perspective on human evolution, which used exclusively would perhaps surprise anthropologists and historians. The concept involves reciprocal altruism and the desire of a small proportion of human beings to subvert this explanation for social behaviour. It has been extensively explored by Adrian Raine the criminologist in a number of books earlier this century.[41]

Is this view genuinely scientific and although widely accepted is the proof genuinely retained in brain imaging? Matthew Cobb, a neurologist, in his work *The Idea of the Brain: the Past and Future of Neuroscience,* [42]denies Raine's perception of the brain and the ability of imaging to discover anything about it (see below) or the pre-frontal lobes in particular. Here, it is proposed that Raine's viewpoint, although acknowledged by psychiatrists and criminologists, is a theory of human nature that does not meet anthropological and historical justification but instead requires an idealised version of human societies, which are both collaborative

---

[41] *The Psychopathology of Crime: Criminal Behaviour as a Clinical Disorder.* Elsevier, 2013
[42] Allen and Unwin. 2020.

and equal. Anyone who steps outside of this ideal is effectively dehumanised by determinants of psychopathology. The range of psychopathology in psychiatric perspectives is much wider then generally suspected and includes chosen and inherited lifestyles common to nomads, for example, travelling salespeople, natural loners, creative types and your run of the mill thug. As in the past lesbians were subject to lobotomy, social misfits, the very people who provide necessary critiques of society, are threatened with extinction.

Adrian Raine has written about the biological roots of crime claiming that crime is due to biological differences, including differences in criminal's brains, and begins his hypothesis with a reference to Lombroso, the scientist (sic) who claimed that criminal behaviour could be seen in the physical characteristics of the face. Personal physical ugliness indicated advanced criminal traits. Lombroso[43] claimed that criminals were lower types, further down the evolutionary chain than people of his class and advantages. The

---

[43] Raine, Adrian. The Anatomy of Violence: The Biological Roots of Crime. Penguin, 2013.

discovery of Neanderthals no doubt aided this view, as the first example was it seemed somewhat heavy boned and apelike as a consequence of age (for his time) and arthritis. More recent examples have shown a different type, more like us. Lombroso also detected an indentation in criminal skulls, of a little brain, that was again ascribed to criminal characteristics. Lombroso went on to create a hierarchy with Jews and Italians at the top and Southern Italians, Bolivians and Peruvians at the bottom. Lombroso was an Italian Jew from the north of Italy.

Although Lombroso is no longer included in the mainstream of psychiatry, and until Raine's limited endorsement viewed with disdain, demonstrates to some degree my claim in recent papers that psychiatry is built on the bedrock of racism.

Now while Raine acknowledges that Lombroso and those that followed his ideas proved a social disaster he nevertheless believed also that somehow they had hit on the biological aetiology of bad behaviour. He provides a list of crimes from murder to wife beating clearly convinced they are the same and have the same source. His understanding, based on data and graphs, exudes the superficial cognitive approach of magazine articles. Step parents are more likely to kill young children in their care, and mothers kill their young children if they lose their partner and need to look for another *resource*, which hardly accounts for the huge number of single mothers in many societies fighting tooth and nail for their offspring.

He brings in evolutionary psychology to show the early behavioural stage of violence, which according to him is based on acquiring resources. Violence here is fixed into the notion of psychopathology, used by psychiatry as a label, but bearing all the hallmarks of a metaphor, a symbolic counterpoint to normality. Raine's understanding of violence has none of the complexity of Slavoj Zizek, seen in his recent book crisply entitled *Violence*[44] , in which he points out that the social and political consequence of violence prevents our thinking about it. Zizek writes: *A dispassionate conceptual development of the typology of violence must by definition ignore its traumatic impact.* Raine positions violence neatly, as psychiatrists do, in the *other*, it is not part of real people but to those he dehumanises. As he and his wife were attacked in

---

[44] Profile Books, 2010.

their flat by an armed burglar he may have sought to deflect the experience by dehumanising his attacker.

Not human

In effect, violent people are not fully human, and certainly not like Raine who *is* fully human. He seems also, unlike the people he deals with, privileged and comfortable in and with life. His upbringing was entitled and provided an easy, compared to some, route to celebrity. Meanwhile, psychopaths appear to be like the Morlocks in *The Time Machine* (1895)-see below- and are an extension of the working class. Raine, like most of us, is uncomfortable with violence and needs to dispose of it by labelling those who do or have employed it. While this is not necessarily a bad thing in itself, it is if it becomes part of systemic or objective violence of the state. Psychiatry as an arm of the state is guilty of this.

Violence, to which he confines much of psychopathology, is clearly not a human trait for Raine. Indeed his notions belong to a liberal viewpoint that H.G. Wells would have been happy to express, although even happier to dismiss as evidence of class structuralism of the middle and upper classes. For Wells, violent people were particularised as Morlock (as above), a group that departed from general humanity. Their traits are or would be determined psychopathic.

Raines, as with most psychiatrists, creates oppositional relationships between those (middleclass English men?) who exist within western civilised values and others who have other significant values. The Morlock represent the working class, living underground, and reversing the usual arrangement with the rich of the time by existing parasitically (for Raines a psychopathic trait although all humans exist parasitically off the flesh of domesticated animals) off the Eloi having effectively domesticated them into farm animals and engaging in occasional culling. The Eloi, an effete form of the upper classes, were thoroughly deprived of violence and effectiveness, indicating thereby that Well's understood that neither group exampled genuine humanity but expressed a symbolic separation of traits. Endorsing only the traits a thinker finds desirable is not perhaps acceptable. Although the Morlock resemble in some measure Neanderthals and for Raine the Munuducu, see below, the

Eloi have become defenceless children and in this work will be further represented by the !Kung in Raine's eyes..

My suggestion here is that Raine is in fact dealing with big issues and does not recognise it or does and desires to appropriate the territory of philosophy. He has minimised issues in order to persuade. For Raine, psychopathology is a coverall term and yet at the same time is indicative of specific traits (2013, 4). Raine conceives of repeated criminal behaviour as demonstrating psychopathic tendencies and yet the nature of crimes is not inclusive, but *exclusive*, including only some crimes. His concept of crime and psychopathology seems rarely to include those who do a range of white collar crimes. His main concern seems to be the physical disruption of society, which he views as an insane or disturbed act. Specifying the nature of different forms of crime is important but Raines places only some under the label of psychopathology, usually violent ones. While violent crimes are disturbing the violence of states is more so, but Raine fails to deal with this as stasis seems for him important. Blue collar crime tends to be publicly displayed, conducted in the open carrying masculine social structures that confirm the masculine traits of the offender, while white collar crimes are done in private inside homes or buildings for greatest concealment. Raines appears to have no interest in the latter or political demonstrations of control.

Raines as with many of his generation of biological interpreters of human nature became inspired by Richard Dawkins' *The Selfish Gene,* which involves the ruthlessness of genes in reproducing themselves. From this excellent beginning, Raine moves from the biological to the mental, and conceives of the selfish genes, which work without obvious intention, into human states of selfishness. Similarly he attributes moral states to animals (2013. 31). Raine continues from seemingly antisocial personality traits to antisocial groups and cultures. Here he introduces two apparently disparate cultures, the !Kung Bushmen of the Kalahari Desert and Mundurucu tribe of the Amazon, again employing the oppositional binomial context common to psychiatric thinking. In effect, employing morality to describe mental states.

Mundurucu

Raine declares that the struggle for resources shaped and shapes human mentality. He advocates in a minimisation of anthropology, geography and history the theory that physical environments provide inherited characteristics, taking us uncomfortably back to a hypothesis of Herodotus and what is often considered the first known expression of racism. He mentions thereby the Bush People of Africa asserting that their harsh environment produced altruism, but showing no awareness that it did not do so for the Arabs in the equally arid characteristics of Arabia whose altruism was limited by clan or tribe. Equally, he does not seem to know that the Bush People were pushed out of their original homelands by the larger Bantu and into the desert. He points to the Mundurucu, who live in a lush environment where everything grows and food is plenty and, who, according to Raine, have developed cheating (very important for Raine based it seems on tropes of possession) or psychopathic traits because life is very easy. They, for Raine, I suspect are the

Morlocks. Cheating there is the result not of a fight for resources, but for an advantage over other males, the attitude that produced the glories of Greece with playwrights for example competing one with another. In fact, this is an expression of a simplistic view of the above disciplines, cherry picking whatever suits his case. The Mundurucu view of women as pollutants, all men staying and sleeping together, can be found in other societies, which are normally described as male dominant-not thereby subject to moral judgements but to the recognition that human cultures exist over a range of behaviours. The pollution taboo tends in some societies to be representative of the cosmos, in which women are central. Simply primitive, or pre-technological societies, are far more complex than Raine imagines.[45] Not knowing enough is not a reason to form a psychological hypothesis that many will take seriously! Hebrew society developed the same or similar ideas that were cogent to them, based on ideas of physical and spiritual contamination, but who also produced a moral philosophy.

---

[45] Mitoo, Das. Menstruation as Pollution: Taboos in Simlitola, Assam*Indian Anthropologist*

Vol. 38, No. 2 (July-Dec. 2008), pp. 29-42

!Kung

The societies created by the !Kung are based on the scarcity of water in the desert, and perhaps concern with outsider intervention. The agreeably instituted marriage ties that Raine indicates were and to some degree still are based on very early marriage for !Kung girls without possibility of choice, little clear emotional development and freedom. The intrusion of Bantu men into the desert has caused greater choice for !Kung girls and women and more varied relationships. [46] An outsider could say the !Kung girls and women now have more control over their sex lives, marry later and perhaps are less subject to early death as a consequence of bearing and rearing children at too young an age and as acting as a future resource for the family. Although many can now be called promiscuous, no matter what Raine believes, they have not turned from altruistic behaviour to psychopathological behaviour. Promiscuity is a choice not a disorder. It is or was never the altruistic paradise Raine claims but one where women bore the price of the

---

[46] Morbeck, Mary, Ellen/ Galloway. Alison/Zihiman, Adrienne. The Evolving Female: A Life History Perspective. Princeton University Press 1996.

simple, unvarying lifestyle. Although considered the *Harmless People* , like the Eloi, this is perhaps a consequence of a limited population and adjustment to their environment and indeed their technological primitiveness.

That the Mundurucu were once head hunters places them firmly in the antisocial bracket, but so too were the ancient Assyrians (who constructed a vast empire and national gods, which helped construct the Abrahamic universal gods), the ancient Celts, and the British in the 19th century who took back to British the heads of native lords, as did American soldiers the heads of Japanese soldiers after World War II. In fact few cultures have not employed head hunting at some point because heads have particular symbolic values. A culture cannot be understood by a few actions. [47]

What is it?

Psychopathology at this point includes charm, promiscuity, and high verbal skills for example-my first thought was Einstein absorbed in his ideas, or Picasso driven by creativity. Sartre of course by these

---

[47] Harrison, Simon. Dark Trophies: Hunting and the Enemy Body in Modern War. Berghahn Books. 2012.

definitions was yet another psychopath. As brilliant as Churchill was, having no apparent interest in sex, he was a constant husband. While many, envious of genius, might agree with the above, think again! Raine decides that Mundurucu behaviour is or was psychopathic, raiding, competitive, nasty to others. Aggression, possibly of any kind is situated within psychopathology, a separate and distinct non-human characteristic that afflects some (in fact many) humans. Using words such as aggressive and competitive seems sufficient, but Raine is seeking really to pathologise and thereby dehumanise certain human traits. Although this is indeed common now, in each failed relationship one or other of the parties is narcissistic, psychopathic or Machiavellian rather than simply accept the relationship failed. Indeed like the ancient Greeks who gave us wonderful drama and poetry, but who were equally or better known for their martial skills.

Now, no genuine anthropologist would define a human culture in this fashion as between differing mental states, one ill and the other well, but simply see them as alternative cultures in the wide variety of human cultures. What Raine wants to do and successfully is create a sense that one is bad and the other good, in a form of thinking that suggests moral involvement and perhaps racism. Indeed, Raine's understanding of the Mundurucu is different to anthropologists who noted a combined patrilineality and matrilineality [48], and their supposed psychopathic aggressiveness ignores their history of local migration and conquest in the Amazon, establishing peace with their neighbours and functioning as mercenaries under the Portuguese authorities. Like the Ancient Spartans they made excellent warriors and survived at times on their capacity for war. Although their aggression could have been culturally based in the unstable ethnic regions of the Amazon in which they lived it gave them protection from other expansionist tribes and may in effect have been a product of acculturation. The violence of the Mundurucu society was directed towards outsiders, was often quite brutal, but child captives were taken into the group and treated well. Conflict between Mundurucu villages was unheard of and there the emphasis was on non-competitiveness and harmony-the traits Raine considers healthy.

---

[48] Murphy, Robert F. Matrilocality and Patrilineality in Mundurucú Society

American Anthropologist
New Series, Vol. 58, No. 3 (Jun., 1956), pp. 414-434 (21 pages)
Published by: Wiley on behalf of the American Anthropological Association

Warfare in effect strengthened the group thereby existing within a constructs of purpose and social development.

Raine's description of psychopathic traits

Psychopatholgy involves unreliable fathers, those for Raines who function like parasites, as with Bantu men and the !Kung women that become their lovers, freeing the women from family and domestic slavery (of a kind). Parasites for Raines, a privileged and entitled professor, do not have jobs, own their own houses and cars, they do not sustain relationships, thereby reflecting the normalcy code Raines works by. My work on the domestication of human beings by psychiatry can be referenced here. The ideal and altruistic society of !Kung mentioned by Raines is also known to be simple, indeed technologically primitive. They are the *Harmless People*, a product of domestication, and thereby normal. Psychopathology is described as producing difficult and rebellious people who refuse to obey society's rules (innovators perhaps?). The men (he talks mainly of men) who possess homes (for psychiatry a sure sign of normality), stay with their children and wife and wives, keep the same job are clearly not psychopathic. They may of course simply be unimaginative and boring types, but for psychiatry that is actually normality as such types are more easily controlled. The emphasis on sedentary lifestyles indicates the connection between domestication and sanity or normality.

Raine brings sexual infidelity into the equation in the same breath as rape and decides that women suffer more from a mates emotional infidelity than their sexual infidelity, a belief that holds to the essential differences between men and women but once again goes against current data[49] , although I suspect this kind of data collection owes much to cultural and generational difference. Raine sees the difference he held as true and scientific as respecting different responses to resources. Basically, his understanding of people is based on their movement to and away from psychopathology. Although no doubt as he writes, a violent man would beat an errant mate close to death if infidelity was discovered, a woman finds a

---

[49] Carpenter, Christopher J. *Meta-analysis of sex differences in responses to sexual versus emotional infidelity*
:Men and Women are More Similar than Different. Psychology of Women Quarterly 2011 online.

way out of such relationships and he seems unable to imaginatively grasp alternatives to the resource concept and consider the power of states of mind such as a man's pride (or woman's for that matter),which true can be seen as a resource reaction, a loss response, childhood experiences of loss and abandonment and living in environments with similar men.

All about gene

Raine continues onto his main concern, that of genes. This after all concerns the genetic nature, biological nature, of psychopathology. He writes on a killer called Jeffrey Langrigan who was brought up by nurturing adopted parents from a very young age but did not emerge into adulthood a well-adjusted individual (a peculiarly American concept encompassing normalcy and conformist constructs in a fashion akin to Raine's own thinking) but became a killer. As while in prison Langrican stumbled across his birth father, in the manner of racy magazine articles, who was also a killer surely it was in his genes. Maybe? But what does Raine really know about Langrigan's upbringing except what he has been told, especially as he earlier devoted many paragraphs to the multitude of dangers to children from step parents or adoptive parents who do not share their children's genes. Raines here again may be referencing class, as the adoptive parents seem to have been middle class and the natural father lower class. Gene theory here and folklore/Old Wife's Tales and gossip meet. In fact, throughout Raine is really talking about the control of others, the Morlocks and lower class, against the backdrop of a perfect society without aggression.

Social control

Looking for and finding simplistic reasons for complex issues seems the function of modern psychiatry. Although Matthew Cobb in *The Idea of the Brain* (2020) states that brain imaging cannot detect aberrations in criminal brains, many researchers hold grimly to this to support their ideas. It may again be a matter of perception whereby what hypothesis declares is true, must be true. Psychotropic drugs worked because pharmaceutical companies said they did and doctors believed them as it provided mental health workers with status and a reputation, although false, for efficacy.

Psychopathology as seen by psychiatry, expressed also within criminology, is that all criminals are psychopaths without any further thought on the matter. Are such concepts really that far from Lombroso or the concepts of my youth that Gypsies and Travellers for example were impulse thieves with no morals-in fact they possess strong moral codes- and yet earlier concepts that all Black men are rapists, all Northern Europeans cold, all Southern Europeans passionate? Are we possibly dealing with a new, equally misinformed social racism (something of a contradiction, I know) assumed by a privileged, entitled group, who usually are white, against underprivileged groups? Have doctors had their brains scanned too? Do they exhibit the same qualities and flaws? In fact Raines admits he has and that his pre-frontal cortex functions in the same fashion as a serial killer, but maybe millions upon millions of others have too and the aberration discovered by Raines and others is simply a distortion of quantitative testing?[50]

---

[50] Lareviewofbooks.org/article/here be monsters Adrian raines the anatomy of violence

Conclusion

Fatalism is a component of such thinking. Predestination joins this sorry group. Those who sit in judgement were predestined to success (forget about the advantages of money and birth, because at worst it corroborates these beliefs). At best, morality has been substituted for psychology: the variables indicate inadequacy as well as antisocial tendencies. Villon, Rimbaud, perhaps even Shakespeare, Lucien Freud, Winston Churchill, Einstein would all have been consigned to the dustbin of life in childhood under the hawk-like gaze of modern psychology and psychiatry.

Raines' concept of *malingering*[51] as a psychopathic disorder (I have not made this up) demonstrates that psychopathology is defined in reference to society and notions of good citizenship, terrible people who pretend to be ill and consequently take time off receiving by default probably the minimum wage doing a difficult job in difficult conditions. It is structured around psychiatry as an arm of the state.

---

[51] *Malingering and Criminal Behaviour as Psychopathology.* Malingering and Illness Deception. Halligan, et al. Editors. Oxford University Press. 2003.

The DSM echoes this kind of thing, exampling a concern with stasis and refashioning quarrels with stasis as expressions of psychopathic disorder. Raine, like many modern biological psychiatrists, sees mental disorders as deviations from a statistical norm, exhibiting clear problems with quantitative investigations into human nature (95)-mistaking this for science. His position, as with many biological psychiatrists is firmly entrenched in comfortable, middleclass understandings of the world. According to the statistics up to 35 % of British males will be convicted of a criminal offence, but what offences and does that include middleclass, white collar crimes? Does he include cheating, not repaying debts or train fares-clear psychopathic traits according to Raines who values the state with its civilised values? Along the way, in his attempt to distinguish anti-social tendencies as also psychopathology based it seems upon concepts of society as ideal and the state benevolent, he visits the inadequacies of criminals in general who rarely marry, usually co-inhabit (such rotters) and exhibit it seems little desire for security or settling down. Through *quantitative methodology*, Raines has discovered that this is the norm and as a result those leading more stable (and dull) lifestyles are normal and others dysfunctional or mentally ill. In biological psychiatry no one acts through choice-except perhaps for the psychiatrist. Those the psychiatrist treats are perhaps on a lower IQ level (sic) and from a lower class than they are and this factor appears to permeate their thinking.

The nature of societies can and probably are determined by the environment and what emerges is perhaps determined by resources but that means organisation, strategies and ideologies with group and individual personalities as expressions of these. These strategies include the acquisition of resources, for example, by elite groups who prevent the rise of other groups through methods of control that involve diagnosis, divide and rule tactics and esoteric knowledge that only they pretend to understand. Throughout his writings Raine alludes to several descriptive works such as the DSM and Jahoda's (96) examples of mentally normal psyches, which often seems to reflect high achievers only with reference to scientific and artistic achievements. At no point does he evaluate these works but accepts them as true.

Groups (professions, trades, etc) often function as tribes expressing shared norms and perceptions, and true in many ways seek to harvest and retain resources which benefit their tribe and kin. Seeing psychiatrists as acting in such a way makes sense of their often ludicrous claims, authoritative tendencies and the carving out of empires.

The reality

Although Raines writes on the evolutionary nature of psychopathology, let's consider a more reasonable view.

Humankind needed certain impulses to evolve in lands with large and very dangerous predators. Those impulses *may* have survived from ape ancestors. Human beings developed strategies, which involved states of mind that functioned to cause death, to fight predators and hunt for large game. They changed with sedentary life and required traits of agreeableness and obedience in order to live in large communities, such as towns and cities, and to control cattle and wheat. The aggressive qualities stayed with us, as did the capacity to think symbolically, often sublimating aggressive aspects through art.

The capacity to fight in armies was a response to both city life and domestication. Now, Raines and his colleagues want to eliminate the more aggressive amongst us who saved human communities in the past, and head human nature towards harmless !Kung and Eloi through the dehumanisation of certain uncomfortable human traits holding thereby that such people form a group apart.

His use of *parasites* to describe such people reflects on him and his group who have harvested a large amount of resources and protect it from the greedy eyes of others not, in Raine's eyes, as clever or entitled as he and his group. Marx used the same word or at least the same idea but for the wealthy and entitled. Nevertheless, Raines like many neurologists and biological psychiatrists is a populariser, not given to deep thought.

***Interventions* (From Simply Psychology)**

It is suggested that intervention should take place with those groups of children most at risk of delinquency, for example those who live in low income families.

Psychopaths are the poor and disadvantaged, not the professionals deciding their fate. But societies do not operate within such clear cut standards, and the suppression and control of others takes many forms.